STEP-by-STEP

SCIENCE

Space

Chris Oxlade

Illustrated by Raymond Turvey and Shirley Tourret

CHILDREN'S PRESS®

A Division of Grolier Publishing

NEW YORK • LONDON • HONG KONG • SYDNEY
DANBURY, CONNECTICUT

8813784

Photographs: Getty Images: page 8, 11 top (Michael Busselle), 24 bottom;
NASA: page 4, 6 bottom, 9, 10, 16, 17, 19 top, 21, 23 bottom, 26, 28, 31; Planet Earth Pictures:
page 7, 11 bottom, 14, 15 both, 19 bottom, 20, 23 top, 24 top, 29; Science Photo Library:
cover, page 6 top (Mark Newman), 30.

Planning and production by Discovery Books Limited
Designed by Ian Winton
Edited by Sabrina Crewe and Helena Attlee
Consultant: Jeremy Bloomfield

Visit Children's Press on the Internet at:
http://publishing.grolier.com

First published in 1998 by Franklin Watts

First American edition 1998 by Children's Press

ISBN: 0-516-20991-4
A CIP catalog record
for this book is available from
the Library of Congress

Printed in Dubai

Contents

What's Out in Space?

We all live on a huge ball of rock called the earth. The earth is a **planet**. To us, the earth seems like a big place. It takes days to travel around it, even in an airplane. But the earth is very tiny compared to space.

We are used to seeing the sun in the sky during the day. The sun is our **star**. It is 93,210,000 mi (50 million km) away from the earth.

The stars that you see at night are much farther away than the sun. There are millions and millions of stars besides our own. Together, all the planets and stars make up the **universe**.

The Moon

The moon is about a quarter of the size of the earth. It circles around the earth all the time. We say that it **orbits** the earth. Each orbit takes just over 29 days.

Craters

If you look at the moon with binoculars, you can see hundreds of **craters**. The craters were made by rocks from space crashing on the moon's surface.

The moon does not make its own light. But one side of the moon is bright because it faces the sun. As the moon moves around the earth, we see different amounts of its bright side. Sometimes we see all of it, and sometimes just a thin crescent.

When we can see all of the bright side, we call it a full moon. It takes two weeks to go from a full moon to no moon at all. After another two weeks, the moon is full again.

MOONGAZING

1. Draw seven circles on a sheet of paper.

2. Look at the moon one evening and draw the shape you see in your first circle.

3. After four days, look at the moon again and draw the shape in your next circle. Is it getting bigger or smaller?

4. Do this every four evenings until you have run out of circles. The shape of the moon in your last circle should be the same as the one in your first circle.

Visiting the Moon

The moon is our closest neighbor in space. It is the only place in space that astronauts have visited. The first time people landed on the moon was in 1969.

This astronaut is exploring the moon in a buggy called a lunar rover.

Gravity

Gravity is a force from inside the earth that pulls things toward it. Because of gravity, everything stays on the ground or falls downward instead of floating around. The pull of gravity works on the moon, too, but it is much weaker. Everything feels lighter on the moon, and astronauts can move in great leaps.

The layer of air around the earth is called the **atmosphere**. The moon has no atmosphere at all. This means that there is no air there. There is no rain to wash away this astronaut's footprints. The footprints could still be there in 10 million years.

A flag was left on the moon by astronauts. There is no wind to blow the flag, so a stick across the top holds it up.

The Sun

The sun is a huge ball of glowing gases. The **gases** give out great amounts of heat and light. The sun gives us light to see by and heat to keep us warm. All growing things need the sun's light and heat. Without the sun, the earth would be a freezing cold, dark place with no living things on it.

The sun is more than a hundred times bigger than the earth. It measures 869,920 mi (1.4 million km) across.

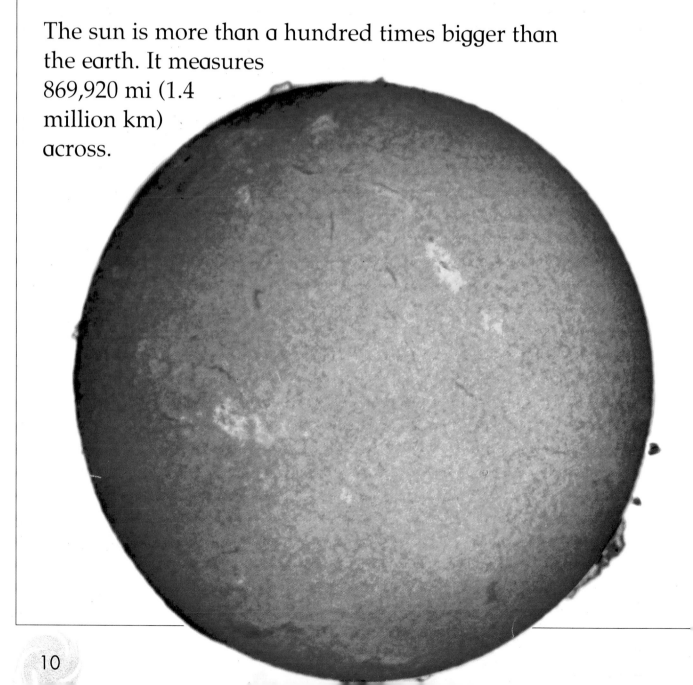

Each day the sun rises in the morning. We see it travel across the sky during the day and set in another part of the sky. It appears to move, but really it is the earth that is spinning around. As the earth turns, we see the sun from a different position at different times of day.

Blackout

Sometimes the moon passes between the earth and the sun, which blocks out the sun. This is called an eclipse. This is a photograph of an eclipse. You can still see the glow of the sun behind the dark circle of the moon.

The Solar System

Just as the moon orbits the earth, the earth orbits the sun. Eight other planets orbit the sun, too. Together, the sun and planets and their moons make up a family called the solar system. The sun is at the center of the solar system. Here you can see the planets in their orbits around the sun.

THE SOLAR SYSTEM

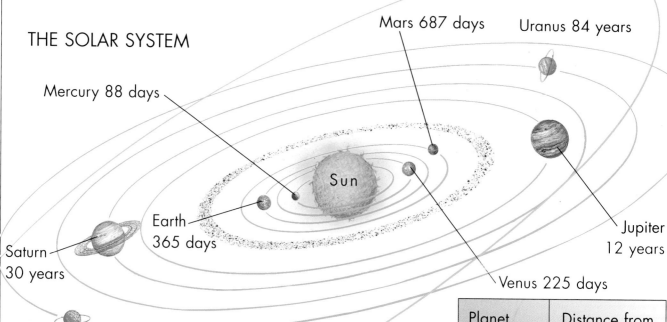

Mercury 88 days

Mars 687 days

Uranus 84 years

Earth 365 days

Sun

Saturn 30 years

Jupiter 12 years

Venus 225 days

Neptune 165 years

Pluto 248 years

Planet name	Distance from the sun (mi)
Mercury	36 million
Venus	67 million
Earth	93 million
Mars	142 million
Jupiter	483 million
Saturn	887 million
Uranus	1.8 billion
Neptune	2.8 billion
Pluto	3.7 billion

The time it takes a planet to orbit the sun once is called a year. You can see here how long each planet's orbit takes in earth time.

MAKE A SOLAR SYSTEM

Making your own solar system will help you understand how big the sun is and how far the planets are from each other.

1. Cut a 12 in (30 cm) circle out of heavy cardboard to make the sun.

2. Use balls of modeling clay to make the planets. Mercury and Mars should measure only just over 1 mm across. The earth and Venus should be about 3 mm across. Jupiter is much bigger than the other planets. It should measure 3 cm.

3. Find an open space and hold your sun up. Give one planet to five of your friends.

4. The distance between the sun and the planets can be measured by taking big strides and counting each one as a yard (meter). The person holding Mercury should take about 13 strides away from the sun. Venus should take 23 strides, earth 32 strides, Mars 48 strides, and Jupiter 168 strides.

5. When you are all in position, look around and see where everyone else is. Look how far Jupiter is from the sun. If you carried on with your model, Pluto, which is 3.7 billion mi (5,914 million km) from the sun would be 0.8 mi (1.3 km) away.

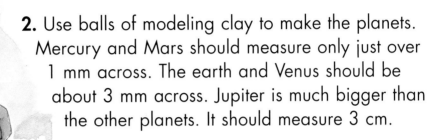

Sun

Jupiter

168 meters

13 m

23 meters

32 meters

48 meters

Mercury

Venus

Earth

Mars

The Inner Planets

The earth is one of the four rocky planets that are nearest to the sun. Mercury, Venus, and Mars have mountains, valleys, volcanoes, and canyons, just like the earth. But they have no air or water, so there are no living things on them.

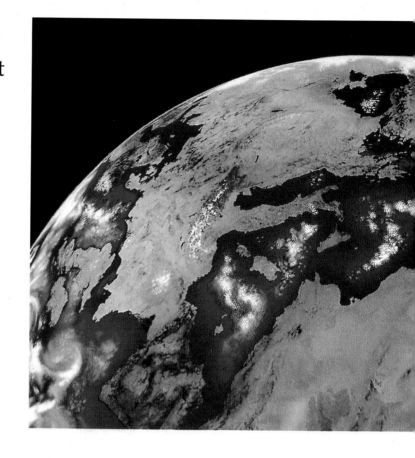

The earth (above) is the only place in our solar system where animals and plants can live. Mercury (left) is nearer to the sun than the other planets, and is very hot during the day. This is the surface of Mercury. It is covered in craters, made by space rocks crashing into it about four million years ago.

Venus is the nearest planet to the earth, but it is very different. The atmosphere on Venus is cloudy and poisonous. It is the hottest of all the planets in our solar system.

The Red Planet

Mars is sometimes called the Red Planet because of the color of the rocks and soil on its surface. It is covered with red dust and has a pink sky.

The Outer Planets

Beyond Mars are four enormous planets that are made of gas
and liquid instead of rock. They are Jupiter, Saturn, Uranus,
and Neptune.

Jupiter (above) is the largest planet in the solar system. It is
very stormy. The red patch you can see is called the Great Red
Spot. This is a storm that has been going on for hundreds of
years. You can also see some of Jupiter's moons in this picture.

Saturn (below) has beautiful shining rings that surround it. The rings are made of millions of chunks of rock and ice. Some chunks are as small as grains of salt and some are as large as a city! Scientists believe that Saturn has 18 moons.

The Smallest Planet

Pluto is the farthest away from the sun, so it is very cold. It is smaller than the earth and made of rock. If we could stand on Pluto, the sun would look like just a bright speck in the sky.

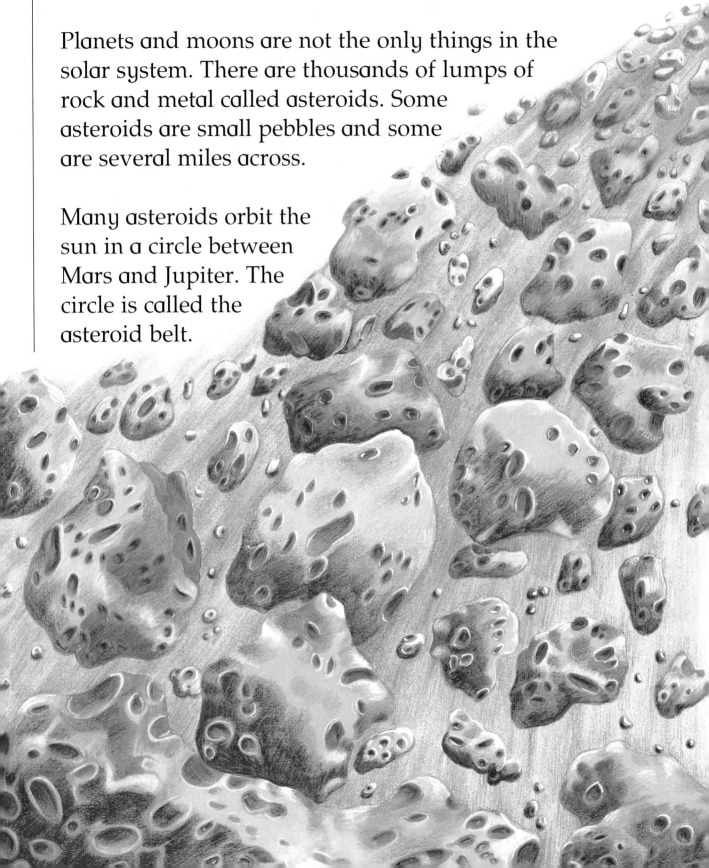

Asteroids, Comets, and Meteor

Planets and moons are not the only things in the solar system. There are thousands of lumps of rock and metal called asteroids. Some asteroids are small pebbles and some are several miles across.

Many asteroids orbit the sun in a circle between Mars and Jupiter. The circle is called the asteroid belt.

Comets are huge lumps of ice and dust. Comets usually orbit far beyond the planets. But once in a while they come nearer to the sun. The comet Hale-Bopp (right) came close to the earth in 1997.

Sometimes lumps of space rock come into the earth's atmosphere. Most of them burn up in the atmosphere, making a streak of light called a meteor, or shooting star. Some meteors hit the earth and make craters in the ground. The crater in the picture above must have been made by a very large meteor.

Stars

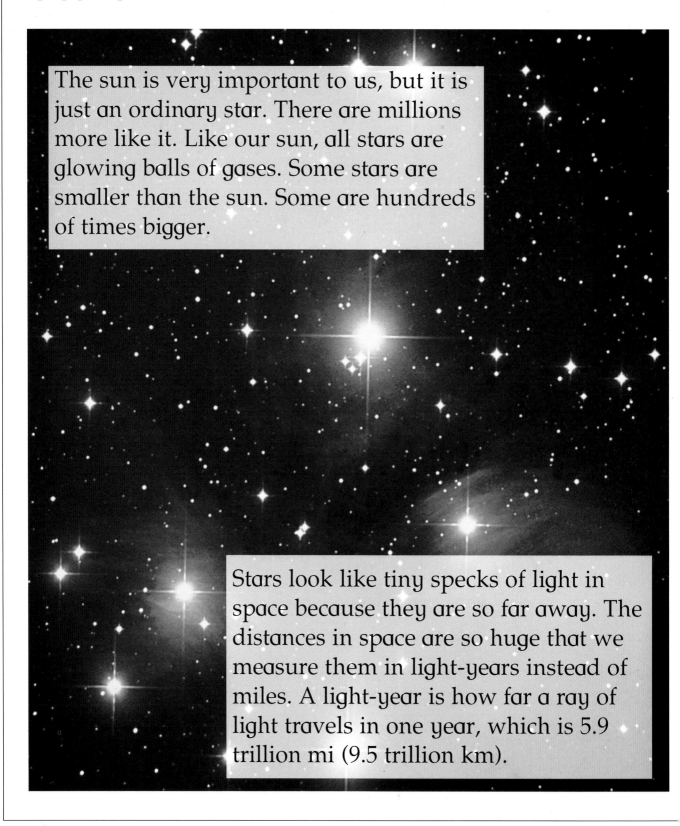

The sun is very important to us, but it is just an ordinary star. There are millions more like it. Like our sun, all stars are glowing balls of gases. Some stars are smaller than the sun. Some are hundreds of times bigger.

Stars look like tiny specks of light in space because they are so far away. The distances in space are so huge that we measure them in light-years instead of miles. A light-year is how far a ray of light travels in one year, which is 5.9 trillion mi (9.5 trillion km).

A Star Is Born

This is a **nebula**. It is a huge cloud of dust and gas floating in space. Sometimes a nebula slowly collapses into a ball. As the ball gets hotter and hotter it begins to shine. After millions of years, a new star is born.

Stars do not live forever. When a star begins to die, it first swells up to an enormous size. It is called a red giant. Usually red giants then collapse, leaving a small star called a white dwarf.

Nebula

Star

Red giant

White dwarf

Sometimes red giants explode instead. These huge exploded stars are called supernovas.

Supernova

Galaxies

A **galaxy** is a huge spinning group of stars. The stars we see at night are in our own galaxy, which is called the Milky Way. The Milky Way is so big that it is hard to imagine. It contains millions and millions of stars. The Milky Way is just one galaxy. There are millions more in the universe!

The Milky Way is shaped like a **spiral**. It measures about 100,000 light years across. Our solar system is just a speck in the Milky Way, about half way out from the middle.

MILKY WAY

Solar
System

22

Sometimes at night we can see another galaxy. It is called the Andromeda galaxy (right), and is over two million light-years away. From the earth it looks like a smudge of light.

Distant Galaxies

This picture shows farther into the universe than any picture has before. It shows a lot of galaxies, but this is just a tiny part of the universe. The galaxies shaped like flattened circles are elliptical galaxies. The ones with no particular shape are called irregular galaxies. You can see some other spiral galaxies like our own.

Looking Into Space

We know about the planets, stars, and galaxies because **astronomers** have studied space. To do this they look through telescopes, which make things seem much closer than they are.

Inside these domes (left) are large and powerful telescopes for looking into space. The telescopes are on a mountaintop because the air is clear and clean there.

This is the Hubble Space Telescope. It is in orbit around the earth. From here it gets a very good view of planets and distant stars. It takes pictures and sends them back to the earth.

Constellations

When you look at the night sky, some of the stars look as though they are in patterns. These patterns are called constellations. Many were named by astronomers in ancient times. They called constellations after mythical beasts, heroes, and gods.

Scorpious

Southern Cross

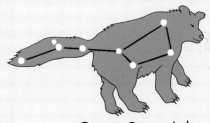

Great Bear (also known as Big Dipper)

Orion

MAKE YOUR OWN CONSTELLATIONS

You can use a cardboard tube and some black paper to make constellation patterns of your own.

1. Cut some circles of paper slightly larger than the end of your tube.

2. With a pin, make small holes in the circles to form patterns of stars. You can use the constellations shown above or make up your own.

3. Stick a circle over one end of the tube with a rubber band.

4. Hold the tube up to the light and look through the uncovered end to see the stars. Put the other circles on the tube one by one to see all your different constellations.

Going Into Space

The stars, the sun, and even the moon are a very long way away. But space itself is quite close. About 93 mi (150 km) up from the earth's surface, the atmosphere runs out and you are in space.

Rockets carry **spacecrafts** up into space. To get into orbit, rockets must be powerful enough to pull away from the earth's gravity. Rockets need big engines and lots of fuel.

The Space Shuttle

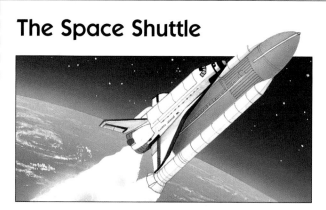

Space shuttles take people and equipment into space. The shuttle is launched into space with two booster rockets. The red tank holds the fuel.

The rockets are dropped back to the earth once the shuttle is in space. The fuel tank is dropped when the fuel is used up.

A BALLOON ROCKET

You will need two or three people to launch this balloon rocket.

1. Thread a smooth piece of string about 26 ft (8 m) long through a drinking straw.

2. Blow up a long balloon, and keep the air in by pinching the neck tightly.

3. Tape the straw along the top of the balloon with some pieces of adhesive tape. Remember to keep pinching the balloon closed.

4. With one person holding each end of the string, slide the balloon and straw along until the neck of the balloon is at one end of the string. Now release the balloon and watch your rocket go!

To get back to the earth, the shuttle slows down and begins to fall into the atmosphere. It glows red hot because it is going so fast.

Now the shuttle flies like an airplane. It glides down to the earth's surface and lands on a runway.

Space Travel

At the moment, we cannot travel to distant planets or stars. The distances are too great. It would take thousands of years to reach the nearest star outside our solar system!

The spacecraft *Apollo 11* took three days to reach the moon from the earth. The **command module** stayed in orbit while this **lunar module** on the right took the astronauts down to the moon's surface.

Space probes can go farther out in the solar system because they have no people on board. Their journeys can take many years. This space probe is visiting Uranus.

The *Pathfinder*
probe landed on
Mars in 1997. It
carried this robot
vehicle, which
drove across the
surface to look at
rocks. *Pathfinder*
sent pictures back
to the earth.

Space satellites are sent into orbit around the earth. Some
send back pictures of the earth and space. Others are used
to send television programs and telephone calls all
around the world.

Living in Space

When you see pictures of astronauts floating around in their spacecrafts, it looks as though living in space is fun. But it can be difficult.

Inside a spacecraft, there is almost no gravity to hold things down. The astronaut's equipment is made so that it does not float away. Even the astronauts are strapped in when they go to sleep!

Solar panels use sunlight to make power

Spacecraft ferries crews to and from space station

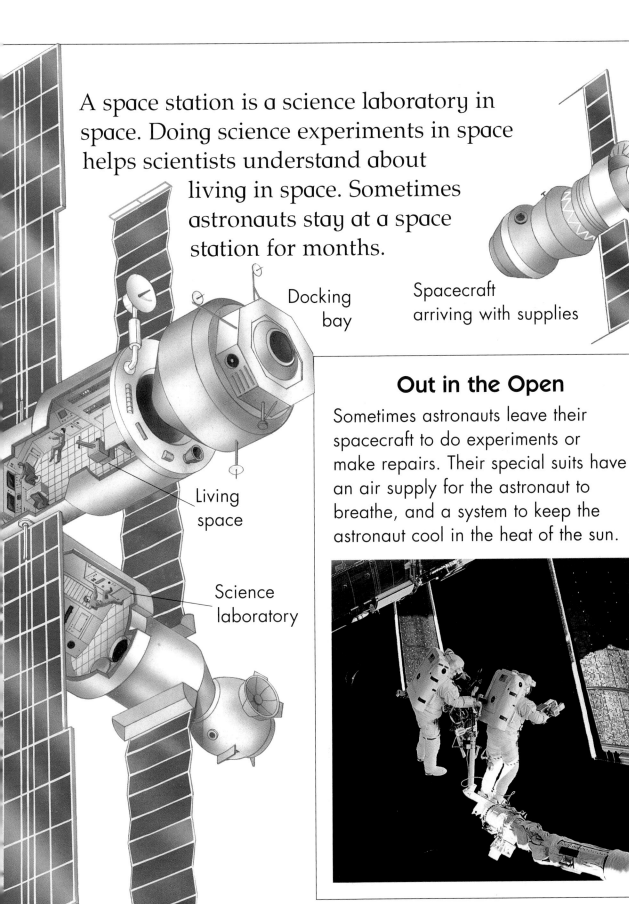

A space station is a science laboratory in space. Doing science experiments in space helps scientists understand about living in space. Sometimes astronauts stay at a space station for months.

Docking bay

Spacecraft arriving with supplies

Living space

Science laboratory

Out in the Open

Sometimes astronauts leave their spacecraft to do experiments or make repairs. Their special suits have an air supply for the astronaut to breathe, and a system to keep the astronaut cool in the heat of the sun.

Glossary

Astronomer: A person who studies space.

Atmosphere: A blanket of gases around a planet.

Crater: Saucer-shaped hole in the surface of a planet or moon made by a meteorite.

Galaxy: A huge group of stars.

Gas: A substance made when a liquid boils. Air is a gas.

Nebula: A huge cloud of dust and gas in space.

Orbit: The path that one object, such as the earth, follows as it moves around another object, such as the sun.

Planet: A large, ball-shaped object which orbits a star.

Rocket: A machine which travels from earth into space.

Satellite: An object which orbits around a planet or moon.

Space probe: A robotic spacecraft which explores a planet or moon in the solar system.

Spacecraft: A machine which travels in space.

Spiral: A shape like a circle which gets smaller and smaller. For example a snail shell is a spiral.

Star: A huge, glowing ball of gas which makes light and heat.

Universe: All the stars, planets, moons, galaxies, and other things in space, and the space between them.

Index